Dave Brubeck

Piano Solos Transcribed by Howard Brubeck

TAKE FIVE

By
PAUL DESMOND

Take Five - 4 - 1

Take Five - 4 - 2

4

Take Five - 4 - 3

Take Five - 4 - 4

IN YOUR OWN SWEET WAY

By
DAVE BRUBECK

In Your Own Sweet Way - 8 - 1

1st Improvisation

In Your Own Sweet Way - 8 - 2

8

2nd Improvisation

3rd Improvisation

12

BOSSA NOVA U.S.A.

By
DAVE BRUBECK

Bossa Nova U.S.A. - 5 - 1

16

Bossa Nova U.S.A. - 5 - 3

KING FOR A DAY

By
DAVE BRUBECK

King For A Day - 3 - 1

King For A Day - 3 - 3

CASTILIAN DRUMS

By
DAVE BRUBECK

Castilian Drums - 2 - 1

Castilian Drums - 2 - 2

THREE TO GET READY

By
DAVE BRUBECK

Light and playful ♩ = 174

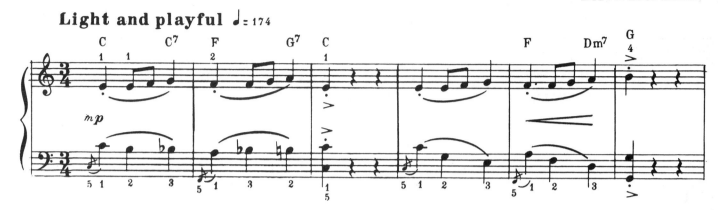

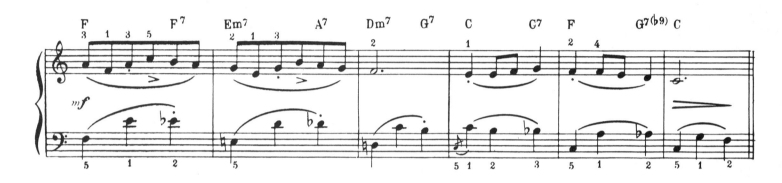

1st Improvisation

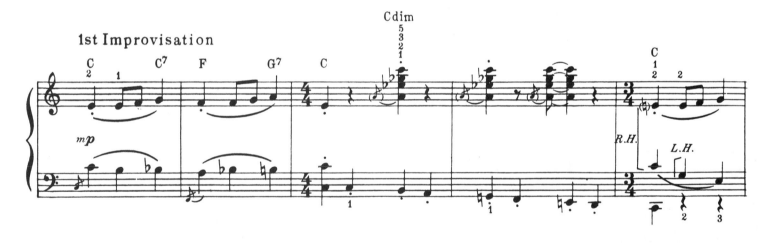

Three To Get Ready - 5 - 1

2nd Improvisation

3rd Improvisation

4th Improvisation

FAR MORE BLUE

By
DAVE BRUBECK

Far More Blue - 5 - 1

30

1st Improvisation

Far More Blue - 5 - 2

2nd Improvisation

3rd Improvisation

Far More Blue - 5 - 5

BLUETTE

By
DAVE BRUBECK

1st Improvisation

2nd Improvisation

3rd Improvisation

4th Improvisation

38

Bluette - 5 - 5

COUNTDOWN

By
DAVE BRUBECK

Moderately fast boogie (♩ = 192)

40

2nd Improvisation

Countdown - 9 - 5

44

3rd Improvisation

CASTILIAN BLUES

By
DAVE BRUBECK

Castilian Blues - 5 - 1

1st Improvisation

2nd Improvisation

3rd Improvisation

Castilian Blues - 5 - 4

4th Improvisation

SUMMER SONG

By
DAVE BRUBECK

Summer Song - 7 - 1

54

Summer Song - 7 - 2

Summer Song - 7 - 3

Summer Song - 7 - 5

*Pedal each chord at the instant of its release.

Summer Song - 7 - 7

MAORI BLUES

By
DAVE BRUBECK

Maori Blues - 6 - 1

1st Improvisation

2nd Improvisation

✱ If the player's hand is small, the lower note of the chords may be omitted.

Maori Blues - 6 - 2

3rd Improvisation

4th Improvisation

Right Hand 8va on repeat

WEEP NO MORE

By
DAVE BRUBECK

Weep No More - 5 - 1

Improvisation

Somewhat faster *(quasi rubato)*
2nd Theme

mf

f

a tempo

PICK UP STICKS

By
DAVE BRUBECK

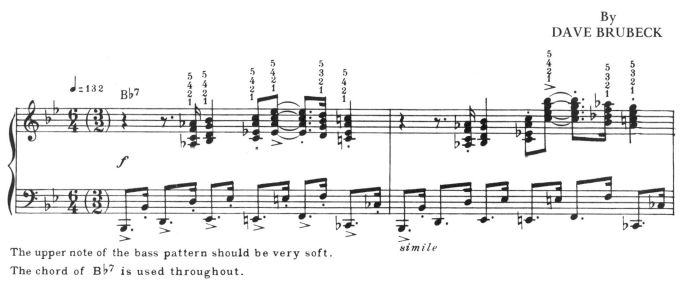

The upper note of the bass pattern should be very soft.

The chord of Bb7 is used throughout.

Pick Up Sticks - 5 - 1

1st Improvisation

2nd Improvisation

3rd Improvisation

R.H. rhythm should be gradually changed to equal eighth notes

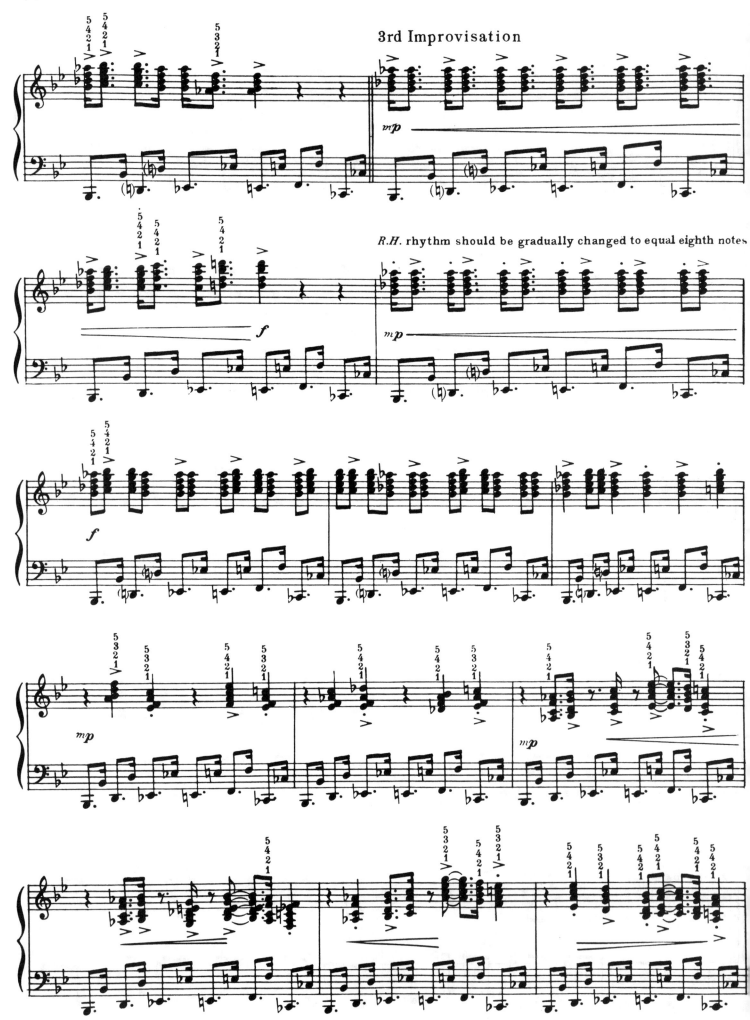

UNSQUARE DANCE

By
DAVE BRUBECK

✱ The hand clapping and drum parts cued in this arrangement are those used by Dave Brubeck and the Quartet in their Columbia recording (CL 1690 - CS 8490). They are included in case the pianist may have help from one or two friends in performance. Without such help, the section from [A] to [B] may be omitted.

Unsquare Dance - 3 - 1

Unsquare Dance - 3 - 2

78

Unsquare Dance - 3 - 3